FROM SEED TO APPLE

Anita Ganeri

Heinemann LIBRARY

www.heinemann.co.uk/library
Visit our website to find out more information about Heinemann Library books.

To order:
☎   Phone 44 (0) 1865 888066
📄   Send a fax to 44 (0) 1865 314091
💻   Visit the Heinemann Bookshop at www.heinemann.co.uk/library to browse
our catalogue and order online.

First published in Great Britain by Heinemann Library,
Halley Court, Jordan Hill, Oxford OX2 8EJ, part of
Harcourt Education. Heinemann is a registered
trademark of Harcourt Education Ltd.

© Harcourt Education Ltd 2006
First published in paperback in 2007
The moral right of the proprietor has been asserted.

Editorial: Nancy Dickmann and Sarah Chappelow
Design: Ron Kamen and edesign
Picture Research: Ruth Blair and Kay Altwegg
Production: Helen McCreath

Originated by Modern Age
Printed and bound in China by South China
Printing Company

13 digit ISBN 978 0 4310 5080 5 (HB)
10 digit ISBN 0 4310 5080 5 (HB)
10 09 08 07 06
10 9 8 7 6 5 4 3 2 1

13 digit ISBN 978 0 4310 5090 4 (PB)
10 digit ISBN 0 4310 5090 2 (PB)
11 10 09 08
10 9 8 7 6 5 4 3 2

The British Library Cataloguing in Publication Data
Ganeri, Anita
From seed to apple. - (How living things grow)
571.8'2373
A full catalogue record for this book is available from the
British Library.

Acknowledgements
The Publishers would like to thank the following for
permission to reproduce the following photographs:
Alamy pp. **10**, **16**, **21** (Vincent MacNamara), **23**
(blickwinkel); Corbis pp. **5** (Paul A. Souders), **7** (John
Bartholomew), **11** (John Heseltine), **14** (Darrell Gulin), **15**
(Patrick Johns), **20** (Patrick Johns), **26**, **27** (Tony
Hamblin/Frank Lane Picture Agency); FLPA pp. **19** (B.
Borrell Casals), **24**; Getty Images p. **12** (photodisc); Holt
Studios International Ltd pp. **13** (Alamy), **22**, **30**;
Naturepl.com p. **17** (Dietmar Nill); NHPA p. **18** (Stephen
Dalton); OSF pp. **4**, **6**, **25**.

Cover photograph of an apple reproduced with permission
of Anthony Blake Picture Library/Maximillian Stock.

Illustrations: Martin Sanders

Contents

Have you ever eaten an apple? 4

Pips and seeds 6

A sprouting seed 8

Leaves and food 10

Falling leaves 12

Apple tree in winter 14

Apple blossom 16

Making seeds 18

Seeds and fruit 20

Insect pests 22

Ripe, red apples 24

Apple picking 26

Life cycle of an apple 28

Apple tree and apple maps 29

Glossary .30

More books to read 31

Index 32

Words written in bold, **like this**, are explained in the glossary.

Have you ever eaten an apple?

An apple is a kind of fruit. An apple grows on an apple tree. The tree grows from a tiny **seed**. People grow apples for eating and cooking.

Wild apples are small and bitter. But apples grown by people are sweet and juicy.

You are going to learn about
Red Delicious apples. You will
learn how an apple seed grows
into a tree, and makes new
seeds and apples. This is
the apple's life cycle.

What is an
apple **pip?**

5

Pips and seeds

An apple **pip** is a tiny brown **seed**.
It is about the size of a grain of rice.
Apple trees grow from these pips.

The middle of the apple is called the **core**. The pips are in the core.

6

The seeds start to grow in the ground. People plant some apple seeds. Some seeds fall out of rotten apples on to the ground.

When does the seed start to grow?

A sprouting seed

The **seed** starts to grow in spring when the weather is warmer. The way a seed starts to grow is called **germination**.

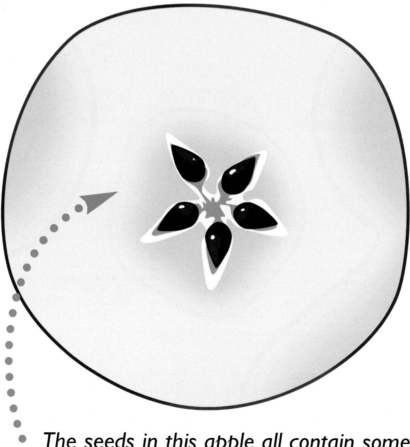

The seeds in this apple all contain some food. This is to help new trees grow when they are planted.

leaf

In the seed are parts that grow into a new apple plant.

shoot

roots

A tiny apple tree plant starts to grow from the seed. The first part of the plant to grow is the **root**. Next a **shoot** and leaves grow.

What are the leaves for?

9

Leaves and food

The leaves make food for the plant. The plant also needs water and a gas (**carbon dioxide**) from the air.

The leaves take in sunlight to help make the food.

The way a plant makes food is called **photosynthesis**. The food helps the plant grow bigger and taller. The young apple tree is called a **sapling**.

What happens to the tree in autumn?

11

Falling leaves

It starts to get cold in autumn. The apple tree gets ready for the cold winter. Its leaves turn red and brown. They fall to the ground.

The leaves change colour and fall off.

12

The buds stay this size until spring.

Small bumps grow at the end of the branches. These bumps are called leaf **buds**. This is where new leaves will grow in spring.

Does the tree have leaves in winter?

13

Apple tree in winter

It is the middle of winter. The apple tree has no leaves. This is because there is not enough sunlight for leaves to make food.

The trees rest through winter.

*Young leaves
need sun
and rain.*

It gets warmer in
spring. The leaf
buds start to open
to show little
leaves. More
leaves grow.

What do the
pink buds open
out into?

15

Apple blossom

Little pink **buds** start to grow among the leaves. The buds open out into lots of flowers. The flowers are small and pinkish-white.

16

Each flower is full of nectar.

The flowers are called **blossom**. The blossom makes a sweet juice called **nectar**. Insects come to the tree to drink the nectar.

17

Making seeds

The apple **blossom** makes a yellow dust. This dust is called **pollen**. The pollen sticks to an insect as it drinks the **nectar**. The insect goes to the next flower.

Bees and other insects like the blossom's sweet smell.

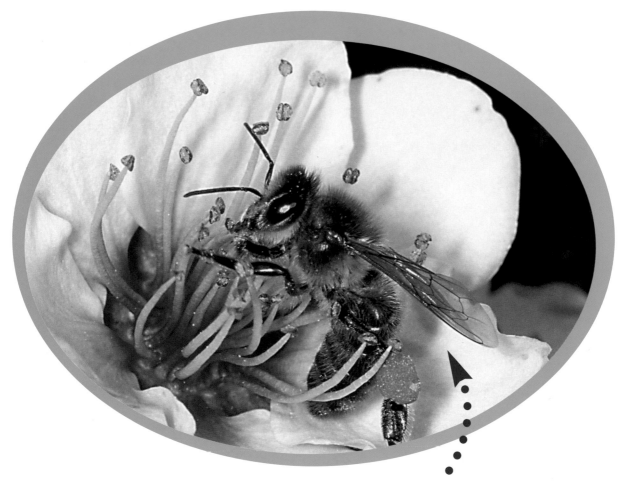

*The bee helps the flowers make **seeds** when it spreads the sticky pollen.*

The insect takes the sticky pollen with it. The pollen joins with parts of the next flower. Lots of new apple seeds start to grow. This is called **pollination**.

Seeds and fruit

The **seeds** are growing so the flower has done its job. Its petals start to droop and fall off. The flower dies.

The petals drop off and leave the middle, where a tiny new apple is growing.

20

Apples are tiny when they are just starting to grow.

Next, tiny green fruits grow around the new seeds. The fruits are the apples you eat. Over the next few weeks, the apples grow bigger.

Why do some apples have holes in them?

21

Insect pests

Many insects eat parts of the apple tree. Caterpillars eat the fruit and leaves. They munch little holes in the apples.

This caterpillar is munching through an apple leaf.

Some farmers spray their apple trees with **chemicals**. This kills the insects so they cannot eat the fruit. But in the wild, apples do not get sprayed.

Wild apples sometimes have holes in them.

Ripe, red apples

It is a warm, sunny summer. The apples are growing bigger and sweeter. They turn bright red when they are **ripe**.

Do you think these apples are ready to eat?

24

*There are hundreds of apples in this **orchard**.*

Soon the tree is covered in
lots of red apples.
The apples are heavy.
The branches bend
under their weight.

When are the
apples ready
to pick?

Apple picking

It is early autumn. The apples growing in the **orchard** are ready to pick. People pick the apples by hand. They pack the apples into boxes.

We pick the best apples. Damaged apples are left on the ground.

*These rotting apples have **pips** which may start to grow in the spring. The apple's life cycle starts again.*

Some of the apples fall to the ground. Birds and insects eat the juicy fruit. The apples left will rot away.

27

Life cycle of an apple

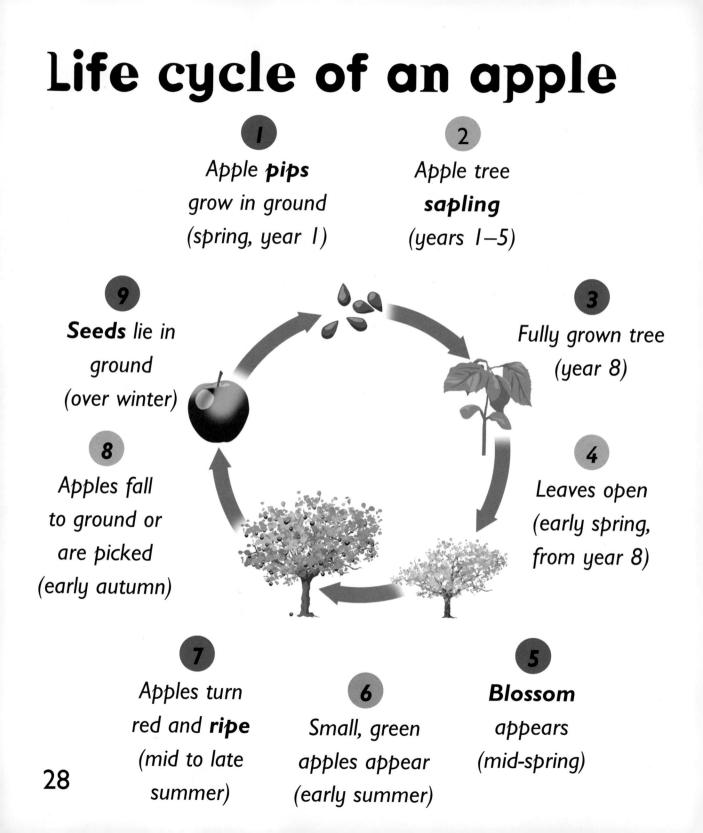

1 Apple **pips** grow in ground (spring, year 1)

2 Apple tree **sapling** (years 1–5)

3 Fully grown tree (year 8)

4 Leaves open (early spring, from year 8)

5 **Blossom** appears (mid-spring)

6 Small, green apples appear (early summer)

7 Apples turn red and **ripe** (mid to late summer)

8 Apples fall to ground or are picked (early autumn)

9 **Seeds** lie in ground (over winter)

Apple tree map

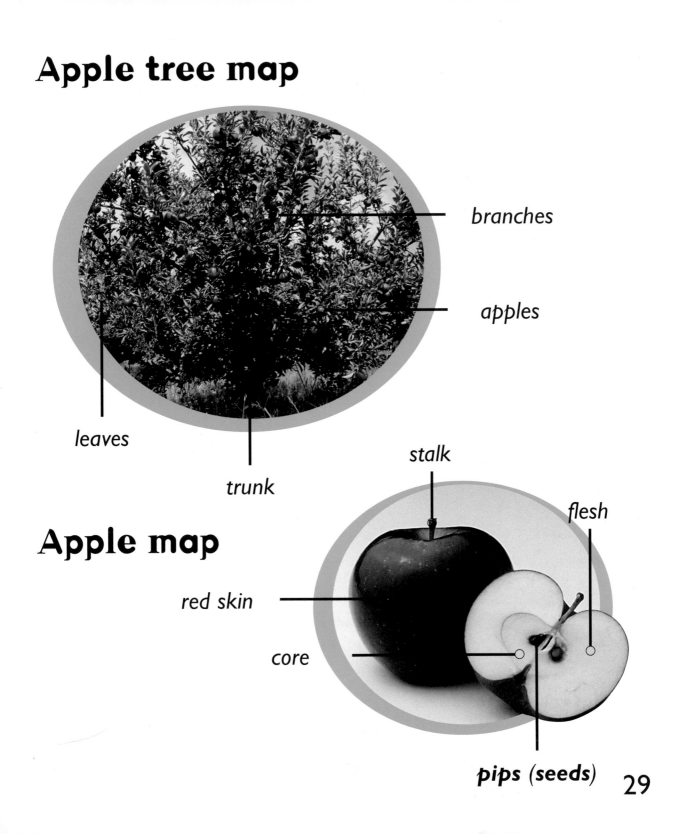

branches

apples

leaves

trunk

Apple map

stalk

flesh

red skin

core

pips (seeds)

Glossary

blossom flowers on a fruit tree

buds parts of a plant that are new leaves or flowers

carbon dioxide gas from the air that plants use to make food

chemicals strong liquids that can kill insects

core middle parts of an apple

germination the way a seed starts to grow into a plant

nectar sweet juice made by blossom

orchard field or garden where fruit trees are grown

photosynthesis the way a plant makes its food from sunlight, carbon dioxide gas, and water

pip apple seed

pollen yellow dust made in a flower

pollination how pollen joins with parts of a flower to make new seeds

ripe fully grown and ready to eat

root part of a plant that grows down into the ground

sapling young tree

seed part of a plant that grows into a new plant

shoot new plant's first stem and leaves

More books to read

Life Cycle of an Apple, Angela Royston (Heinemann Library, 1998)

Life of an Apple, Clare Hibbert (Raintree, 2005)

Nature's Patterns: Plant Life Cycles, Anita Ganeri (Heinemann Library, 2005)

Websites to visit

Have a look at this website to find out more amazing facts about tree life cycles:

http://www.realtrees4kids.org/

Disclaimer

All the internet addresses (URLs) given in this book were valid at the time of going to press. However, due to the dynamic nature of the internet, some addresses may have changed, or sites may have ceased to exist since publication. While the author and publishers regret any inconvenience this may cause readers, no responsibility for such changes can be accepted by either the author(s) or the publishers.

Index

autumn 11, 12, 26, 28

blossom 16, 17, 18, 28
branches 13, 25, 29
buds 13, 15, 16

cores 6

fruit 4, 21, 22, 23, 27

leaves 9, 10, 12, 13, 14,
    15, 22, 28, 29

photosynthesis 11
pips 5, 6, 27, 29
pollen 18

roots 9

seeds 4, 5, 7, 8, 9, 19, 20,
    28, 29
shoots 9
spring 8, 15, 28
summer 24, 28
sunlight 10, 14

winter 13, 14, 28